Exploring a Theme: Beliefs in Action in the World

The theme of beliefs in action in the world is an important one for RE. Children can learn a lot from exploring the practical actions believers make in response to their religious beliefs and values. Such actions can also be challenging and influential in children's own moral and spiritual development.

The activities in this book aim to help you explore such beliefs and actions with children. Each article focuses on one or more religions, but all activities can easily be applied to others. Each suggests a strategy. Faith stories are used as a starting point for reflection with younger children on the theme of kindness, generosity and the value of each person. The global themes of poverty, environment and justice are introduced for older primary pupils by means of a WebQuest and case study activities. Each section identifies the importance of using effective stimulus materials in order to get children thinking and doing, and of careful planning of opportunities for children to express their own ideas. Links to assessment are provided in each section in the form of pupil-friendly 'I can' statements.

We hope you enjoy using these activities and that they will stimulate your own ideas for others.

Joyce Mackley
Editor

RE Today weblink: www. retoday.org.uk

The RE Today website provides some free additional resources and classroom ready materials for subscibers. Look out for the 'RE Today on the web' logo at the end of selected articles.

The password for access can be found in each term's *REtoday* magazine.

Giving: exploring two faith stories about generosity and kindness towards others

For the teacher

The two faith stories featured in the following activities share a common theme. They both teach that God is pleased when people show kindness and generosity quietly to others.

The activities using the two stories, one from Christianity (The Widow's Mite) and one from Islam (The Two Brothers), enable younger primary children to

- retell religious stories and suggest meanings for actions

- reflect on some of the ways in which people can show kindness and generosity quietly to others

- talk about why these are good ways to behave.

The two main strategies suggested – a visual learning approach and a pupil talk activity – can be adapted and applied to a wide range of RE content and contexts.

The activities have been planned to

- engage children's active participation

- meet Religious Education learning objectives

- contribute to meeting Early Learning Goals for personal social and emotional development, and knowledge and understanding of the world, and for aspects of literacy for 5–7 year olds.

I can ...

The following pupil-friendly criteria could be used to assess children's responses to the activities. Level 1 describes what most 6-year-olds should be able to do; L2, what most 7-year-olds should be able to do.

Level 1

- **Tell someone what happens** in a story Jesus told or in a story from Islam.

- **Say what I think** is good about sharing things and being kind to others.

Level 2

- **Retell** a story Jesus told / a story from Islam and **say what it tells me** about sharing and kindness.

- **Ask some questions** in response to stories from religions about kindness and generosity, **giving my own answers.**

Information file
Faith stories

A Christian story: The Widow's Mite
Mark ch.12, vs41-43

- In New Testament times widows were often very poor, having no male to provide for them. Despite this, the widow in the story demonstrates her quiet devotion to God by giving generously of what little she has.

- For Christians this teaches that the essence of all true giving is sacrifice. Jesus saw self-giving love as characteristic of God and recommended it to his followers as a practical basis for action.

A Muslim story: The Two Brothers

- Giving sadaqah – voluntary payment or good action for charitable purposes – is one of the five basic duties of every Muslim. It should be done quietly, without any advertisement.

- The two brothers give in the best possible way – in secret, under cover of darkness.

Christianity: The story of the Widow's Mite
(Mark ch.12 vs41-43)

For the teacher
Ways of using the story

- One visual way of telling the story is by use of a web-based PowerPoint such as that available from the 'Sermons4Kids' website (details in the See also box). The excellent child-friendly artwork is downloadable for schools to develop their own PowerPoints for this and other Christian stories.

- Revisit parts of the story and ask some probing questions to encourage personal response and reflection on the themes of kindness and generosity.

- Role-play the story in groups of three: two children taking the role of the rich people making a big show of giving money, the other taking the role of the widow quietly giving. Record actions using a digital camera. Display images on a whiteboard, talk about the feelings and motivations of the characters, add key words to images. Talk about why Jesus told this story.

- Select an appropriate picture showing a key moment from the story as a stimulus for follow-up work. Add speech bubbles to structure children's paired/group talk. The example on page 4 asks children to identify two things they notice in the picture and four things to think about. Ask children to talk about how they would complete the speech bubbles. After 5–10 minutes, ask children to share their responses and compare their own answers to those of others.

See also
Website: www. sermons4kids.com/ hmartin.htm

PowerPoint slides retelling the story of the Widow's Mite, featuring the excellent artwork of Henry Martin, can be downloaded from Sermons4Kids for school and church use.

Note: This is a Christian website designed for use in church and some of the focus questions in the PowerPoints will need to be changed for classroom use.

The story of the Widow's Offering

Faith story

One day Jesus was sitting in the temple. He was watching as people dropped money into a large collection box.

A group of rich people threw in large amounts of money. What a clatter it made! What a lot of noise and fuss they created! They were very pleased with themselves, making a big show so that everyone noticed how much they had given.

A little later on, a poor lady, whose husband had died, came along. She was all alone in the world, with no one to love and care for her. Her clothes were old and tatty. She had very little to eat. Quietly, she put two very small coins, worth only a fraction of a penny, into the collecting box. Head down, she hurried away, hoping that no one had noticed her.

- *Which of these do you think Jesus was most pleased with? Why?*

Calling his disciples to him, Jesus said, 'I tell you the truth, this poor widow has put more into the treasury than all the others.'

- *What do you think Jesus meant?*

- *Do you think the lady was a kind person? What makes you say this?*

- *What sorts of things can we do to show love and kindness?*

© Henry Martin

3 We think the lady is feeling.........

wondering.......

3 Some things we can GIVE to help others are........

2 We think this picture shows.........

© Henry Martin

5 We want to ask about.....

1 In this picture we can see........

4 We think Jesus is feeling.....

wondering.......

Islam: The story of the Two Brothers

4–7

This is a story about two grown-up brothers who owned a farm. One was married and had children. The other was single. They shared all the work, and at harvest time they divided the crop in half. Each brother had his own barn in which they stored the grain.

One night after a busy day harvesting the corn and bagging it into sacks, the brother who lived alone, sat down, thinking happily about what a good harvest it had been. He felt very satisfied with all their hard work, and looked forward to taking it easy now most of the work was done.

But then a niggling thought passed through his mind. 'Here I am,' he thought, 'just with myself to think about. My brother has a wife and family to feed. It's not fair for me to keep half the corn – he should have a larger share than me.'

He knew that his brother would never agree to taking more, so he came up with a secret plan!

'I know,' he thought, ' When everyone's in bed tonight, I will move some of my sacks into his barn. No one will see me in the dark!'

So that night he did just that. Slowly, secretly, he moved six sacks into his brother's barn.

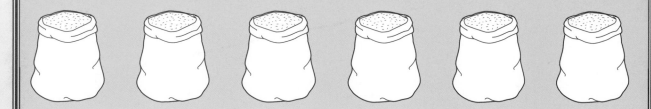

Later that night the other brother lay awake, also thinking about the harvest. 'I'm so lucky' he thought, 'I have a lovely wife and family, the farm and lots of food to eat. My brother is all alone. I wish I could do something for him. What could I do?' He lay awake thinking ... and then suddenly came up with a bright idea! 'I know' he thought, 'I could give him some of my corn!'

So he crept outside and took six bags from his own barn and put them in his brother's!

The next morning the two brothers got up for work as usual. Imagine the surprise when the unmarried brother went into his barn! 'Why are there so many sacks of corn in here?' he wondered. 'I thought I'd moved some last night. I must have been dreaming!'

Then the married brother went into his barn and he couldn't understand it either. Neither of the brothers said anything because they wanted to keep quiet about giving the corn, but they didn't understand what had happened. And neither of them ever found out!

Traditional Muslim story

For the teacher

Ways of exploring the story of the Two Brothers with younger primary pupils

Pupil talk and record activity

- Retell the story using the outline on page 5. Pause in appropriate places for children to participate and respond.

- Revisit parts of the story and ask some probing questions to encourage personal response and reflection on the themes of kindness and generosity.

- Put children in pairs with a talk partner. Ask pairs to talk about these questions:

  - Do you think the brothers in the story were kind and caring? How do you know?
  - Why did they give the bags of corn in secret?
  - What sorts of things can we do to show we care for others?
  - What sorts of things can you share with others?

- Give each pair a barn outline (enlarged to A4 size) and six 'sack' shapes. Ask pupils to

  - Retell the story of the two brothers inside the barn shape.
  - On each of the six 'sack' shapes write and draw things you can share with others. Stick these on the barn outline.

- If possible invite a Muslim visitor – perhaps a mum or dad from your school – to tell the children about *sadaqah* (voluntary giving or good action for charitable purposes). Talk about why it is better to do things for others quietly without advertisement – like the brother giving secretly in the story.

 Weblink: photocopiable pages to support the activities on pages 3–6 are available for download for subscribers on the RE Today website: www.retoday.org.uk

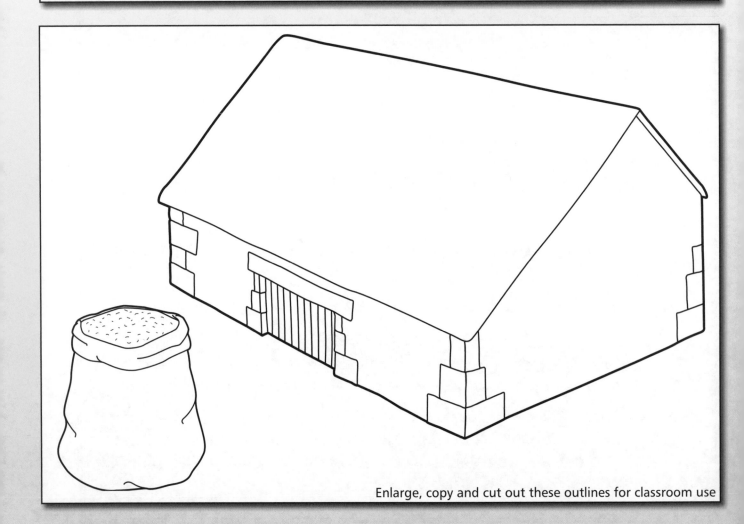

Enlarge, copy and cut out these outlines for classroom use

Everyone matters – exploring some stories from the life of Jesus

For the teacher

In Religious Education, storytelling is a powerful tool as it:

- develops the imagination and allows children to see from another's perspective

- helps children learn about the experiences and beliefs of others

- can enable children to reflect on how they behave and how they treat others.

In this section three stories have been chosen to illustrate how Jesus responded to three types of people who needed help:

- The **poor** – the story of the blind beggar Bartimaeus (Mark ch.10, vs 46-52; Luke ch.18, vs 35-43)

- The **stranger** – the story of the Roman centurion's servant (Luke ch.7, vs 1-10)

- The **outcast** – the story of Zacchaeus (Luke ch.19, vs 1-10).

Through sharing these particular stories, children can learn that for Christians, Jesus showed that God loves everyone – no matter who they are or what they have done.

The activities aim to enable children to

- **reflect** on people who need help in their community

- **think** about how people are treated today

- **understand** that Christians try to follow the example of Jesus by helping people who are in need.

I can ...

The following pupil-friendly criteria could be used to assess children's responses to the activities. Level 1 describes what most 6-year-olds should be able to do; Level 2 describes what most 7-year-olds should be able to do.

Level 1:

I can....

- **remember and tell someone** three things that happened in the stories shared

- **use some religious words** to talk about the stories

- **talk about** my own experiences and feelings connected to feelings in the story.

Level 2:

I can....

- **retell a story** about Jesus and **say what the story might mean** to a Christian

- **suggest** two things a Christian might do to follow the example of Jesus in helping people

- **Ask and respond** sensitively to questions about my own and others' experiences and feelings.

See also

For advice and guidance on the use of 'stilling' and 'guided visualisation' activities in RE see either

- *Reflections*, ed Rosemary Rivett (RE Today Publications, 2004, ISBN 978-1-904024-07-1).

- Mary K Stone, *Don't Just Do Something, Sit There* (RMEP, 1995, ISBN 978-1-85175-105-1).

Jesus heals a poor, blind beggar
(Mark ch.10, vs 46-52; Luke ch.18, vs35-43)

For the teacher

- **Guided visualisation** is a technique that helps children to enter into a story using their imagination. Children are provided with the opportunity to think through the thoughts, feelings and experiences of the characters in the story and then explore their response to the story through a carefully planned activity.

- It is important to ensure that children feel secure and comfortable before the story is shared and that ground rules are carefully negotiated before the activity.

- Most guided visualisations begin with a '**stilling exercise**'. Children are asked to sit comfortably but with alertness, aware of both feet resting on the floor and their hands on their knees. The teacher talks them through a process of attentive listening, firstly listening to sounds outside and then inside the room until finally focusing on listening to themselves – focusing on their own breathing. When children are ready, the teacher invites them to participate in the story or 'journey' she is to take them on in their imagination.

- The following script for such a 'guided visualisation' uses the story of Jesus healing a poor, blind beggar. It aims to engage children in reflecting on what the story says about how Jesus treated people in need. Children are asked to imagine themselves 'seeing' the story from the blind beggar's point of view.

Jesus heals Bartimaeus – a guided visualisation script

Another day, it is just another day.

Sitting by the roadside. I cannot see anything. I am so hungry. I wish I had some food.

I can almost taste my favourite food. *What would that be if you could choose?* (Pause)

The sounds I hear are the same as always. *Listen … what can you hear as you sit there by the roadside?* (Pause)

But then, I hear a new sound. What can it be? It is getting louder and louder. I think it might be cheering. I can feel the rush of people passing by.

I hear people say it is Jesus. I have heard people talk about him. He does wonderful things.

I believe he can make me see. I'm sure he can help me.

I call out to him. *What do you call out? What do you want to say to Jesus?* (Pause)

I hear a man speak to me. His voice is gentle and quiet. It makes me feel different inside.

The man asks me what I want. *What do you say to him? How do you feel?* (Pause)

I say I want to see again.

I hear Jesus say 'Go, You are healed, because you believed.'

My eyes seem strange, but as I look, I see the man called Jesus.

I can see so many other things. I turn around and around to see everything.

What can you see? What do you notice most? (Pause)

I notice so many things and see so many colours. I jump for joy and praise God.

Thanks to Jesus, my life has changed for ever! *How do you feel now? What do you want to do next?*

Sit quietly for a moment. When I tell you, I'd like you to go quietly to your table and be ready for the next activity.

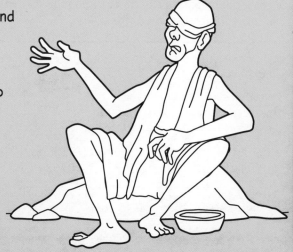

For the teacher

The life of the poor blind beggar in this story was transformed by the faith he had in Jesus.

The following activities are designed to help children express the thoughts and ideas they had during the 'guided visualisation' and to enable them to

- retell the story of Jesus healing the blind beggar, using senses and emotions
- talk about how the blind beggar felt before and after he met Jesus
- ask questions about the experiences and feelings in the story.

5-7

Children could do one or more of the following, from the point of view of Bartimaeus.

Provide all materials on the children's tables in advance

Bartimaeus's favourite food

What do you think this might be?

Draw and label some pictures to show this.

Sounds by the roadside

What could you 'hear'? (*Would there be cars then? What animals might there be? What sounds would they make? [Suggest a donkey – make a braying sound.]*)

Jesus is near

Imagine you are the blind beggar. What do you call out to Jesus?

Using a children's version of the Bible, read the question Bartimaeus asked Jesus.

Why did you say this?

Seeing

What could you see when your eyes were opened? What did you notice most?

Make a picture to show these.

(What do they think someone who had been blind would notice the most? Encourage children to identify colours, shapes, faces...)

Feelings

How did you feel before Jesus came along?

How did you feel after he had helped you see again? Use card to make faces to show these feelings.

A senses poem

- This exercise is an excellent follow-up to a guided visualisation and can also be done using a video clip, poster or picture.
- Children imagine they are a participant or bystander in the story or the scene depicted.
- Using the following frame, they write a six-line poem on what they see, hear, touch, taste, smell and wonder (one line for each). The lines have been arranged below to match the order of experiences in the guided visualisation. This basic format can be adapted and made as simple or as complex as you require, depending on the age and ability of pupils. Invite pupils to share their poetry with others.

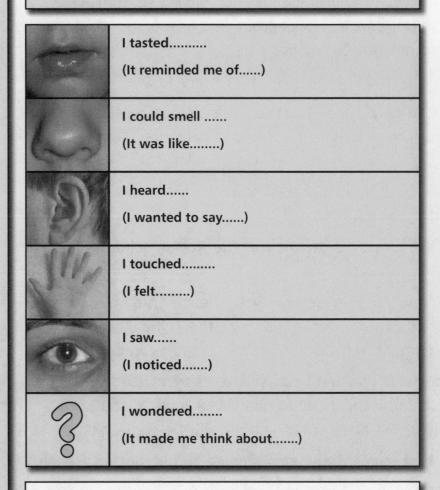

	I tasted.......... (It reminded me of......)
	I could smell ...... (It was like........)
	I heard...... (I wanted to say......)
	I touched......... (I felt.........)
	I saw...... (I noticed.......)
	I wondered........ (It made me think about.......)

 A downloadable version of this senses poem framework is available for subscribers on the RE Today website.

Jesus helps a stranger – the Roman centurion
(Luke ch.7, vs1-10)

For the teacher

The activities in this section focus on the story of Jesus helping a Roman soldier, someone who was, at that time, often hated as an enemy. The activities can be used to help children think about what we can learn from Jesus about

- treating people as individuals
- being kind and caring towards those who may be rejected by others.

Information file

- At the time of Jesus many Jews hated the Romans who had invaded and occupied the land of Palestine.

- The centurion in this story is shown to be a kind, respectful man. He goes out of his way to help a trusted servant. He has shown respect to the Jews by building a synagogue for them, and shows respect to Jesus.

- Jesus looks at the person – not the uniform – and is impressed with the centurion's personal faith and kindness.

Jesus heals the Roman centurion's servant

Jesus went into a city. An important man in the army, an officer in charge of 100 men, had a servant who was very poorly. The servant was in a lot of pain and could not get out of bed.

Some friends of the centurion came to see Jesus.

'Please help', they begged. 'This Roman centurion is a good man. He is kind to us and helps us. Please help him.'

Jesus said he would go straight away to see the centurion's servant.

Before he got to the house, the Roman soldier came out to meet Jesus.

'I'm not good enough for you to come into my house,' he told Jesus. 'Please just give the order and I know my servant will be healed. I know you can do that.'

Jesus was amazed because the army officer had so much faith and trust in him. Jesus said to the army officer, 'Go home. Your servant will be well again.'

At that moment the man started to get better. He sat up, got out of bed and began to move around. It was a miracle!

The servant had been healed because his master had so much faith and kindness.

For the teacher

Enlarge the statements below and print them onto cards. Ask pupils to:

- Pick out any cards which reflect what
  - the centurion did in this story
  - Jesus did in the story.
- Next ask pupils to write about some of these inside an enlarged outline drawing of the centurion and of Jesus.
- Next, ask each child to pick two cards for themselves. In pairs, talk about how they could put these into action themselves, e.g. make others feel happy, make others feel better. Ask children to write their ideas inside the child-shaped outline (copied and enlarged!). Make a wall display for the story.

5-7

cared for other people	was kind to someone he did not know	did what people asked him to do
listened to other people	made others happy	spent time with people
made someone feel better	helped someone in need	was unkind to people he did not like

Jesus helps an outcast: Zacchaeus the tax collector
(Luke ch.19, vs1–10)

For the teacher

- Zacchaeus was a tax collector who worked for the Romans at the time of Jesus. He was disliked and distrusted by his neighbours. His life was changed when Jesus showed him some kindness.

- One visual way of telling the story is by use of a web-based PowerPoint such as that available from the 'Sermons4Kids' website (details in the See also box). The excellent child-friendly artwork is downloadable for schools to develop their own PowerPoints for this and other Christian stories.

- Revisit parts of the story and use the following poetry, role-play and talk activities to get children thinking about the characters and reflecting on the themes of saying sorry and making a new start.

See also

- The story of Zacchaeus retold for younger pupils can be found on page 8 in *Exploring Leaders and Followers*, ed. J. Mackley (RE Today Publications, 2006, ISBN 978-1-904024-87-3).

- PowerPoint slides retelling the story of Zacchaeus, featuring the excellent artwork of Henry Martin, can be downloaded from www.sermons4kids.com/hmartin.htm for school and church use.

Zacchaeus

The crowds gathered,
Jesus was coming,
Zacchaeus was scared.

The crowds shouted,
Jesus was here,
Zacchaeus was scared.

The crowds watched,
Jesus was amongst them,
Zacchaeus was scared.

Then something happened!

The crowds gasped,
Jesus had spoken,
Zacchaeus had changed.

The crowds wondered,
Jesus had spoken,
Zacchaeus had changed.

The crowds fell silent,
Jesus had spoken,
Zacchaeus had changed.

Paired role-play and talk activity

Activity 1   Look and tell

Paired talk activity: Saying sorry

Talk about a time when you had to say 'sorry' to someone.

• What had you done? • How did you feel? • What happened when you said 'sorry'?

Talk about a time with a friend when someone said 'sorry' to you.

Artwork activity

• On a big piece of paper make a picture to show what you think happened when the poem says:

'Then something happened!'

Paired role-play and talk activity:

Scaffold the talk: well-designed talk activity cards such as those below will help support both adults and children to stay on task and keep the talk options quite open.

Activity

5-7

For the teacher

Enlarge, print and cut out the role cards below .

Step 1: In pairs give one child card 1 (Zaccheus) and the other child card 2 (person in the crowd). Talk through the activities for each character. Ask pairs to role play the action.

Step 2: Feedback ideas from pairs to the rest of the group

Step 3: Give each pair card 3. Ask them to think and talk about the questions on the card. Ask children, as appropriate, to share ideas with the whole group in a follow up circle time type activity.

Step 4: Using a 'think book' children record some of their ideas from the 'talk session'.

1   You are Zacchaeus, the tax collector

Talk to a partner ... **say** how you are feeling when:

• you are pushing through the crowd to see Jesus

• Jesus speaks to you

• the people say nasty things about you

• Jesus comes to your house.

Now **say** what you do next and why.

2   You are a person in the crowd

Talk to a partner ... **say** why are you there to see Jesus.

Say how you feel when

• you see the tax collector

• Jesus talks to him

• Jesus goes to the house of Zacchaeus.

Say what you do next and why.

3   Now be yourself

Take turns to think and talk about the following:

• How does it feel to be left out?

• Why are people cruel to one another?

• What can you do to help someone who does not have many friends?

Using ICT to explore Christian action against poverty in the world (WebQuest)

For the teacher

- This unit focuses on using ICT and experiential approaches to explore how one Christian agency, Christian Aid, puts the teachings of Jesus into practice today by caring for those who are in need.

- Using real life stories of children living in poverty, the activities invite pupils to ask 'what if it was me?'

- The use of a structured and sharply focused WebQuest together with experiential techniques to stimulate the imagination and emotions aims to engage the intellect and develop the whole child.

I can ...

The following pupil-friendly criteria could be used to assess children's responses to the activities. Level 4 describes what most 11-year-olds should be able to do.

Level 3

- **describe** some things Jesus said about caring for others, **give some examples** of how Christians put this into practice today and **say how this makes a difference** to people's lives.

- 'put themselves in someone else's shoes', say what that person needs and **suggest how** these needs might be met.

Level 4

- **understand** what Jesus taught about caring for others, **give examples** of how Christians put this into practice today and **reflect** on what influences their own responses to people in need.

- **identify** the qualities needed to take action to do what is right and good.

Information file

What is a WebQuest?

A WebQuest is defined by a specific structure

which consists of **five basic elements:**

- **introduction**
- **task**
- **process**
- **evaluation**
- **conclusion.**

The basic methodology remains the same whatever the topic, age group or abilities of the pupils. The structure is extremely adaptable as the level of challenge can be adjusted, for example by:

- **introducing** a more controversial topic
- **varying** the range of sources
- **providing** varied levels of guidance.

It is also adaptable to groups of different sizes. The outcomes can be simple (achievable in one lesson) or complex (taking several lessons to complete).

See also

Further **information and examples** of webquests:

- **WebQuest Portal:** http://WebQuest.org

Some recommended **faith-based websites** suitable for use by children:

- **Global Gang** (Christian Aid)

  www.globalgang.org.uk

- **Islamic Relief** (a UK-based Muslim charity)

  www.islamic-relief.com/submenu/Kids/kidzone.htm

DVD teaching pack resource

- 'We're Changing Our World' – DVD teaching pack for 7–11s from Christian Aid.

  www.christian-aid.org.uk/learn/schools/changingworld/index.htm (look in primary teaching resources)

(All websites and links are correct at the time of publication but may be subject to change over the period this publication is in print.)

Designing a WebQuest –
exploring a Christian response to poverty

For the teacher

This section will take you through the stages of designing a WebQuest which helps pupils to:

- **find out** about, **identify with** and **reflect** on the lives of children in poor countries;

- **apply** their understanding of the teaching of Jesus about caring for others; and

- **evaluate** the difference one agency (Christian Aid) makes to the lives of poor people when it puts these Christian beliefs into practice.

Once you are clear about the **RE objectives** the WebQuest will address, you can begin to build the task. As it is a 'quest' you can be as **creative** as you like! One example of a 'quest' is provided here to get you started. The activities for children to follow are set out 'step by step'. Ideally the process would be available online for pupils to access from their computers.

The **best format** for a WebQuest is to keep the whole process **online**. The WebQuest structure also works successfully when integrated with conventional teaching approaches and resources, as long as the five key stages are followed: 1 Introduction; 2 Task; 3 Process; 4 Evaluation; 5 Conclusion.

7-11

1   The introduction

- All WebQuests open with an **introduction**.

- The purpose of this is to **engage** pupils' interest and attention and 'hook' them into the task. This might take the form of a **real life story, role-play scenario, controversial key question**, or a **problem** or **mystery** to solve. Two examples :

The simple statement of a key question:
- Why should people who follow Jesus care about people who are poor, hungry and badly treated?

or

Real life story: Eboku's dilemma
Eboku and his sister don't live with their parents in their home village in Uganda. They live in a camp nearby where there is a school. They only see their mum twice a week when she comes to visit them. Eboku's mum has the virus HIV and his dad died of HIV-related illnesses when he was just six. Eboku is torn between looking after his mum and looking after his own future by getting an education.

What should Eboku do?

How can Eboku get an education and look after his mum?

©Christian Aid/Caroline Waterman

2 The task

This section makes clear exactly what the pupils will produce as a result of the activity, and the tools they can use to achieve this. The outcome might take the form of a decision, speech, presentation, article, piece of persuasive writing, solution to a problem, creative work, and so on.

The point of a WebQuest task is that it will not allow pupils to simply regurgitate information but requires them to process, synthesise and apply it in a new way. Pupils must move beyond simply telling the teacher what they have found out.

Try using the following task and WebQuest with your class. It uses the Christian Aid children's website 'Global Gang' but the process can be applied to other websites, for example Islamic Relief.

What should... do?

Your task is ...

Use the Global Gang website to **prepare a presentation** which introduces your classmates to the story of one child who lives in very poor conditions. Your presentation should help them to

- **imagine** what it would be like to be that person
- **identify** some things that would help that person
- **understand** what Christian Aid is doing to help

and

- **say why** Christians want to help people in need.

Follow the steps: Step 1 ... Step 2 ... Step 3 ...

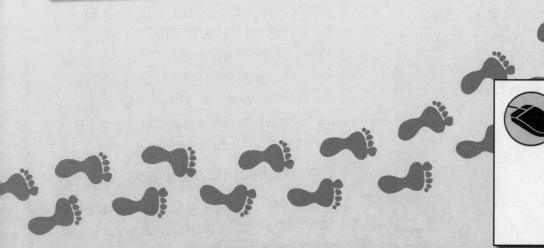

RE Today Website resources:

The materials relating to this task can be downloaded by subscribers from the RE Today website

www.retoday.org.uk

3 The process

The process sets out **how pupils should go about** completing the WebQuest task. This is presented in a number of **steps** so that pupils know how to organise and manage the task. You can prepare **additional guidance and resources** to help pupils make useful notes or structure their learning more purposefully.

One of the defining features of the WebQuest process is that it can only be completed in **collaboration** with other members of a group, and in order to achieve this each person (or pair or sub-group) is given a specified role to play. Individuals become responsible for one particular aspect of learning about the topic and become 'experts' in that area.

7–11

Step 1   One person's story

- **Use the Christian Aid Global Gang website** (www.globalgang.org.uk) to **find and read** stories of children living in very poor conditions in different parts of the world today.

- Go to 'search' on the Global Gang home page. Type in the names of the following children to read their stories.

  Mahamadou, 7, lives in Mali (northwest Africa)

  Sara, 8, lives in Bolivia in South America

  Gile, 10, lives in Bangladesh

  Mario, 11, lives Guatamala

  Wa Moo Paw, 11 is Burmese

  Eboku, 15, lives in Uganda.

- With a partner, **choose one story to think and talk about.**

- **Ask yourselves 'What if that were me?'**

  Talk about the following, making a note of your ideas:

  'If I was .... (name of child in story)
  the worst thing in my life would be ...
  the best thing in my life would be ...
  I would need ...
  I would want ...
  I would feel ...
  I would wonder ...

- **Create a poster or PowerPoint** to present the story and your ideas to the class. **Think about** ways you could design this to make it more interesting for the reader. Do you want to give it an original heading and include a photograph of the person whose story it is? Do you want to use speech bubbles to show your thoughts? Do you want to include questions for your audience to think about?

Step 2   What can be done to help?

- Return to the website (http://www.globalgang.org.uk)

- **Find and list some practical things** Christian Aid does to help people like those in the stories on the website. Click on the button on the home page to find out more.

Step 3   Why should people who follow Jesus care about people who are poor?

- Christian Aid puts into practice the teaching of Jesus. **Read two of the things Jesus said** about helping people in need.

- Go to Bible Gateway website: http://www.biblegateway.com/

- Type in the Bible reference and select 'Contemporary English Version' from the drop down list.

Matthew ch.25, vs31-46 – The story of the Sheep and the Goats

- Highlight the text, right click to save, copy into another document (right click 'copy').

- **Read the story carefully.** Highlight verses 35-40. **Explain to a partner** what you think these words would say to someone who follows Jesus today and what they might do as a result.

- **Design a poster** to show what Jesus said and what Christians could do today.

Matthew ch.6, vs2-3 – Jesus teaches about giving (Sermon on the Mount)

- Highlight the text, right click to save, copy into another document (right click 'copy').

- Read carefully.

- **Make up a catchy slogan or newspaper headline** to sum up what Jesus is saying here. Type it into your document – make it 'eye catching' (e.g. use WordArt and colour).

4 Evaluation

Having clear **evaluation criteria** is an **integral element** of the WebQuest. Ideally the evaluation criteria should be presented in a pupil-friendly form in line with the criteria for different levels of achievement of the syllabus being followed. This will enable pupils to **identify** what they have learned and **evaluate** how well they have met the challenge of the task and what they would need to do to improve. You might also want to provide criteria in relation to identified **key skills** such as communication or working in a group. Relevant **ICT criteria** could be used to make judgements in relation to use of ICT. The WebQuest format opens up opportunities to develop effective **self- and peer-assessment** in RE.

I can...

Level 3

* 'put myself into someone else's shoes', identify what that person needs and suggest how these needs might be met.

* describe some things Jesus said about caring for others, give some examples of how Christians put this into practice today and say how this makes a difference to people's lives.

Level 4

* identify the qualities needed to take action to do what is right and good.

* understand what Jesus taught about caring for others, give examples of how Christians put this into practice today and reflect on what influences my own responses to people in need.

7-11

5 Conclusion

The conclusion **summarises** what the pupils have learned by completing the WebQuest. It should relate to the **RE learning objectives**. This is also a place where you can add any additional thoughts or links to extend pupils' learning to a wider or different context.

Congratulations!

By completing this task, you have shown that you are able to:

1 **Understand** what Jesus taught about caring for others and give examples of this in action today

2 **Imagine** what it might be like to be in someone else's shoes and **show a good understanding** of their feelings, needs and hopes.

3 **Think about** qualities that are needed to take actions that are right and good.

4 **Share your ideas** and findings with others in a clear and informative way.

Well done!!

Hindus and Christians: changing the world

For the teacher

- These lesson ideas aim to bring some sparkle and challenge to the topic of beliefs in action in the world by introducing simply some faith-based charitable action that addresses problems of the environment, poverty, homelessness and war.

- These issues are complex, but here are some subtle and interesting ways of provoking a response from 7–11s.

- Activities for younger or lower achieving pupils can be found on pages 24 and 25. Pages 21–23 are more challenging, suitable for older primary or more able children.

- The device of telling stories of the impact of these problems on your pupils' contemporaries enables some simple, direct connections to be made. Use these four questions to start children talking:

  - *Does every child deserve to live in a world that is fair, just and green?*

  - *What needs to change to make this happen?*

  - *What are Hindus and Christians doing to help make this happen?*

  - *What can we do to change the world?*

I can ...

The following pupil-friendly criteria could be used to assess children's' responses to the activities:

I can...

Level 3

- describe how a religious charity tackles a problem of suffering.

- make a link between what I believe in and what I do.

- make a link between religion and action.

Level 4

- show that I understand the impact of a religious belief on the actions some people take to deal with problems of suffering

- apply my own ideas about suffering to the problems of fairness, environment and/or homelessness.

**Classroom activity:
Spotlights on the problems children face around the world**

Activity

- Use the 'spotlight' drawing on page 21 (there is a colour version of this on the RE Today website, which subscribers can download for free).

- Make a copy for every pupil. It can also be projected onto a whiteboard. This will be a key tool for their work on these topics.

- Begin by asking pupils in pairs to make four lists of the problems children would face if they had:

  - Not enough food

  - An environment that is being destroyed

  - No proper home

  - A war that is frightening them.

- Next ask them to suggest what needs to be done to lessen or solve these problems. Encourage them to make many suggestions in reply to each of these. This could be done as a role-play: if you were the Prime Minister or President of the whole world for one week, what would you do about these problems? (Again, there is a worksheet that structures this task to download from www.retoday.org.uk for RE Today subscribers.)

- Discuss the results of the children's thinking as a whole class, and vote on which ideas are the best. You could record this voting on an IWB programme that makes bar charts.

Spotlight on some world problems

- The picture shows four problems that some children face today.
- Talk about the questions with a partner and fill in the boxes with your thoughts and ideas.
- Decide which questions you need more information about and where you might find this.

7-11

What's the problem here?				
How would you change the world to make this problem better?				
How have Hindus and/or Christians 'shone a light in the darkness'?				
Is this a good example of Hindus and/or Christians changing the world? Why?				

Four stories of Hindu and Christian action to help those in need

The story of Pandurang Shastri Athavale
Hindu beliefs in action

Pandurang Shastri Athavale was born in 1920, near Bombay in India. He loved to learn the *Bhagavad Gita*, an important Hindu holy book. When he grew up, he became known all over the world for his knowledge of this great scripture. He could have gone anywhere but he was concerned about his own people in India. There was great poverty in the villages. The environment was spoiled by carelessness. He was puzzled: he wondered if the beautiful truth of the Gita could be shared with the ordinary people of India. He decided to give his life to that cause. Living by his teachings, his followers, called Swadhyayees, have transformed the lives of thousands of people.

Here are three of their many achievements:

- Farm land is bought to share, set aside, and be worked by Swadhyayees. They believe work is worship. The crops are given free to anyone who needs them.

- For Pandurang Shastri's followers, trees are a sign of God. Volunteer groups of villagers plant and care for orchards on barren desert land. They see this as worship, devotion to God. The environment is saved for the future and fruit is given away free to anyone who needs it.

- In fishing villages, his followers set aside money regularly to buy a 'floating house of God'. This is a fishing boat for the community. People can use the boat freely. Fish caught from this boat are given away to those in need.

Shompa's story
Christian and Hindu beliefs in action

In 1977, five young Hindu women in a small village in Bengal decided they would like to change their world. In their village there were many hungry people, not enough education and not many chances for women to change their lives.

The five women set up Sundarban Khadi Village Industrial Society. SKVIS asked Christian Aid in Britain for help. SKVIS is a Hindu organisation. This is a good example of Hindus and Christians working together.

Shompa is a girl whose life has been changed by SKVIS: she has been given the chance to go to school, has learned dance, drama, reading, writing, numeracy and craft skills. She now works caring for her family's goats and cows. Shompa is one girl whose life was changed by SKVIS and Christian Aid. There are many more like her.

For the teacher

Shompa Lives in India, by Jean Harrison (1999, ISBN 9780904379402) is a super big book from Christian Aid. The book is available to buy from a range of sources.

Probhadan's story
Hindu and Christian beliefs in action

Probhadan's parents died when he and his brother were only three and five years old. They were homeless, and no one cared for them. They made a little money by the incredibly dangerous task of catching snakes, which could be sold to a hospital so that their venom could be used to make serum for anyone who was bitten.

Probhadan says 'I always tried to catch the most poisonous snakes, because we got more money for them.' He wore a small 'Aum' symbol, a sign of Hindu belonging, which he had kept from his mother when she had died. 'I think the Aum kept me safe: I was never bitten,' he says.

Probadhan's life was changed when he was given a home at an orphanage which had been set up by a group of Christians from England. In 1879 ten young men from Oxford had decided that they wanted to change the world. They travelled to Calcutta (now known as Kolkata) and worked with the local people to set up a home for children living on the streets. Today, 130 years later, it is still there.

Probhadan lived at the orphanage for 15 years. He learned to play the violin, and took classes in metalwork, textiles, book-keeping and management. He now has a successful life in Kolkata.

A story from the life of Vinoba Bhave
Hindu beliefs in action

Vioba Bhave was a friend of Ghandi. He lived in India in the middle of the last century, at a time when the army was fighting landowners in a vicious war. Many children died in the fighting. Vinoba stood for peace.

People respected his wisdom and often came to ask for his advice. One group who came were 40 poor families, 'Harijans' or Dalit people, as they would be known today. They were outcasts who were only allowed the worst jobs. They said they did not want to fight, but with no land they would die of starvation.

Vinoba listened to them and was deeply moved by their desire for peace. He called a prayer meeting that afternoon. Thousands came. Vinoba told the story of the Dalits and asked: 'Is there anyone who could solve this problem?'

A deep, spiritual silence fell. Then a local rich man stood up. 'I will give them 100 acres of land' he said. Vinoba could not believe his ears. He thought this was a sign from God. The Dalit leaders refused to accept the 100 acres: 'Eighty will be enough for us,' they said.

It was the beginning of Vinoba's way of making peace. He called on landowners to give land to the poor rebels, and thousands did so. He was given hundreds of acres every day, over 100,000 acres of land in all. He told people 'God wants you to give away land. It will bring you spiritual treasure.' Peacefully, one acre at a time, he changed India for good.

7-11

Why is the cow so special in Hinduism?

Information file

- In India cows are loved, protected and cared for. In big cities they may live roaming the streets, and if a cow comes to your house, you would take it as an auspicious, happy sign of blessing and feed it. Cows are not just treated kindly and gently, but reverently.

- Mahatma Gandhi said: 'Cow protection is one of the most wonderful phenomena in all human evolution, for it takes the human being beyond his species. Man, through the cow, is enjoined to realise his identity with all that lives. Cow protection is the gift of Hinduism to the world.'

- Hindus in Britain may revere the cow too. At Bhaktivedanta Manor, in Hertfordshire, members of the Krishna Consciousness movement have been running a cow protection scheme for nearly 30 years. The cows pull traditional ploughs to cultivate the land, and calves are suckled by their own mothers. They are never sold or slaughtered, but are treated with love. 'Cow day' (Gosthastami), a festival in November, is celebrated, and there are vegetarian cooking classes.

Where do you seek your God?

Overlooking him in various forms, in front of you?

He serves God best who is kind to his creatures

Swami Vivekananda, 1863–1902

Photo: Focus Multimedia

Whoever sees the one spirit in all, and all in the one spirit, from then on cannot look with contempt on any creature.

For the teacher

Activity

- These snippets of information contrast sharply with much Western farming practice.

Classroom activities

- The following sayings and the poem provide a start for conversation and for pupils' own poetry about the earth. Literacy might explore the metaphor of earth as mother.

- The photocopiable activity sheet on the next page aims to stimulate pupil talk and response (downloadable from the RE Today website for subscribers)

A Poem for the Earth

Earth is the mother of every thing that lives.
Firm, solid earth, to us all she gives
Kindness and care, for every single day
Food, drink, light, air, to help on our way.

When we dig or pick her fruit
When we take and eat
We should never hurt or harm
Never gouge too deep.

Mother Earth, you cared for us
We will care for you.
Mother Earth is generous
We'll be generous too.

This poem is based on Hindu scripture (the Atharva Veda). It was first published in *Whose World is it Anyway?* ed. J. Mackley and C. Johnson, RE in Practice, RE Today, 2000).

Activity: Something to talk about and do

Probing questions for conversation and written work:

In pairs or groups, discuss these questions and then complete a version of the wheel for yourselves. Compare your ideas with those of others.

- Is it wrong to harm a cow? Why?

- What things to eat come from the cow?

- Would it be good to thank the cows for their milk? How could you do that?

- Do we own cows, or do they own themselves, or does God own them?

- What is your favourite animal in all creation? Why?

- How can we show better in future that we love the world?

- What is your wish for the world, to make a better world for the future?

- What 'thank you' would you like to say for the world of nature? Who to?

- What do you think 'the creator' (God) would say about how we treat the world?

- What would you like to ask 'the creator' (God) about the world and how it is made?

7-11

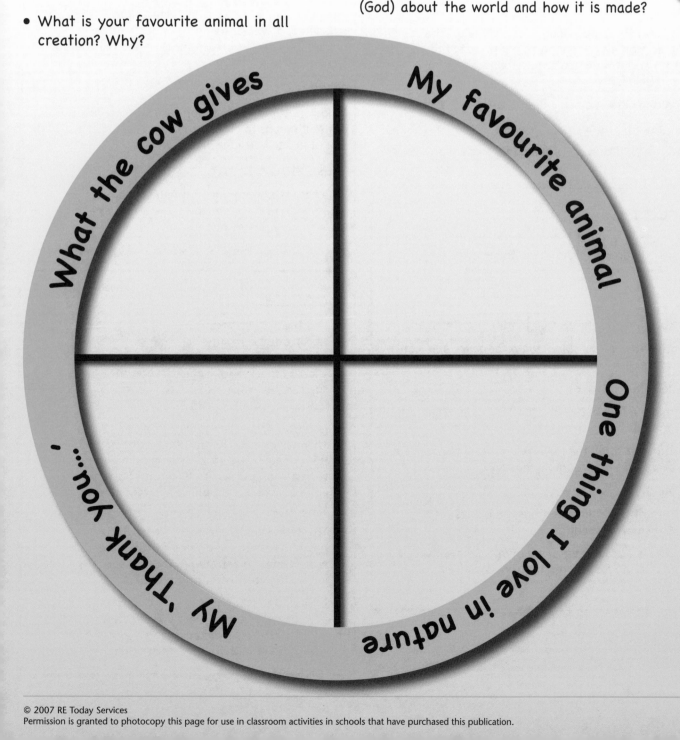

Standing up for peace and justice

For the teacher

John Sentamu hit the headlines in August 2006, not because he was an archbishop, but because he chose to act out in a very public way his concern for peace and justice.

He believed he was responding faithfully to the teaching of the Bible, and in a long tradition of 'prophetic enactment'. Isaiah, Ezekiel and Jesus, among others, had all 'acted out' their message, God's message, to draw people's attention to it, despite any personal consequences.

Using John Sentamu's actions as a stimulus, the activities in this section aim to engage older primary pupils in thinking about the impact on self and others of acting on your beliefs.

- Can one person make a difference?
- Are actions stronger than words?
- What would they be prepared to take action about?

I can ...

The following pupil-friendly criteria could be used to assess children's responses to the activities:

I can ...

Level 2

- **suggest** two things that matter to a Christian
- *talk about why standing up for peace and justice matters*.

Level 3

- **make a link** between a teaching of Jesus and how it might have an impact on a Christian.
- *suggest some things people do to work for peace and justice, and some things I do.*

Level 4

- **describe and link up** Christian beliefs with Christian behaviour.
- *create a statement of my own beliefs about peace and justice, referring to ideas from Christianity.*

Activity 1
What's it all about?

Activity

This activity enables pupils to practise the important skill of speculation, in considering the meaning of an image. The photograph is also available from the Diocese of York's website (see below).

Activity 2   Why did John Sentamu camp out in the cathedral?

This thinking skills 'Mystery' activity provides a challenging way of trying to understand John Sentamu's actions in a supportive and collaborative context.

Activity 3   Blog spot

'Blog spot' provides an opportunity to reflect on what it means to stand up for what you believe, and for pupils to consider their own responses.

Case study: John Sentamu

The case study of John Sentamu on page 29 can be used to support any of the three activities above, or as a stand-alone resource.

See also

- **The Diocese of York**
  Check out the royalty-free images of John Sentamu (see 'Resources') – ideal for full colour presentation to support the activities outlined here: www.dioceseofyork.org.uk

- *Religion Around Me*, ed. J. Mackley, Exploring a Theme series (RE Today, 2007, ISBN 978-904024-96-5), pages 20 and 21, presents an interview with a young Christian (Religious Society of Friends) who is very much an activist: www.retoday.org.uk

- **Thinking skills in primary classrooms**
  A useful resource database for thinking skills approaches and strategies (not RE-specific): www.standards.dfes.gov.uk/thinkingskills

Acknowledgement
We are grateful to the *Sunday Times* for permission to publish extracts from an article about John Sentamu published on 20 August 2006.

What's it all about?

© Martin Sheppard / Diocese of York

9-11

Activity 1

Work with a partner.

1. Look closely at the picture – write down 5 things that you notice.

2. What puzzles you? Write down 5 questions you have about the picture.

3. Join up with another pair. Share your ideas – what do you think this picture is all about?

Activity

Mysteries – a thinking skills strategy

For the teacher

How do 'mysteries' support learning in RE?

'Mysteries' are very powerful strategies for differentiation and challenge and are also superb tools for diagnostic assessment. They are extremely useful in RE, as well as other areas of the curriculum.

Mysteries are useful for:

- **sorting** relevant from irrelevant information

- **interpreting** information

- **making links** between different bits of information

- **speculating** to form hypotheses

- **checking, refining** and **explaining**

- **talking** about learning and thinking processes through expressing responses to the 'working as a detective' analogy.

Activity 2
Why did John Sentamu camp out in the cathedral?

Activity

In advance of the lesson, print the statements needed for the mystery (pages 30 and 31), including the key question, and prepare enough packs for one for each group of 3–4 pupils.

Explain to pupils that they will be given a question to answer, and a series of clues. **The task** is to identify what they think is a sound answer to the question, based on the clues they are provided with. Point out to pupils that it is the quality of their thinking that is important in the activity, not necessarily a 'right' answer.

Working in groups of 2–4, pupils:

- **Empty** their card pack, and identify the central question which they have to answer. This should remain visible at all times, as a guide and prompt to thinking.

- **Study** the 'clues' on the cards and move them around the table, **discussing, deciding, explaining, refining** their ideas as part of the thinking process. Pupils work to find a **plausible** answer to the question.

- **Respond** to the teacher, who mediates to encourage pupils to **justify** the reasons for their views as they emerge during the activity.

- **Contribute** to a whole class **discussion** and **debriefing** activity, focusing on how the activity helped pupils in their thinking (metacognition). Suitable prompt questions might include:

  - How did you start the task? How did you move on?

  - How did your group work together? Did you disagree? If so, how did you resolve it?

  - What was hard about the task? Why?

  - Did you reject any of the information? Why? Why not?

  - How could this way of thinking help you produce a piece of written work?

  - If you did the activity again, would you do anything differently? Why?

Putting beliefs into action: John Sentamu (newspaper article extract)

John Sentamu, the 97th Archbishop of York, knelt motionless in silent prayer in front of his two-man tent in York Minster.

He planned to spend **seven days** living inside the tent, **fasting and praying** for the situation in the Middle East to improve.

It all started as he was watching a TV news report. In a Lebanese village **an eight-year-old girl** had lost an eye and did not yet know that both her parents and brother were dead. In an Israeli village **an 85-year-old woman** sat alone in her flat, the only person left to hear the rockets screaming through the night.

John Sentamu said:

'I was gutted at that news report … I thought that girl could be my niece, that woman my mother … then I realised that this was what I had been trying to hear. **I was hearing the voice of God in that little girl, in that old woman.'**

So … he cancelled his holiday and moved into the tent!

9-11

He also **shaved his head – a symbol of hope** in Uganda, where the archbishop was born. He said: 'I am trying to say that actually life does have a chance of regrowing, that out of the chaos and cheapening of life in this conflict, there is still hope.'

John Sentamu wasn't the first to **'act out'** a powerful symbolic message he believed was from God.

- The **prophet Isaiah** wandered around naked as a sign that the people would be stripped of their land unless they stopped being corrupt.

- The **prophet Ezekiel** walked around Jerusalem with bags on his back as a warning that people were about to be sent into exile.

- **Jesus** rode a donkey into Jerusalem as a sign of humility.

(published with the permission of the Sunday Times)

Mystery – Why did John Sentamu camp out in the cathedral?

John Sentamu was born in 1949.	John Sentamu decided to fast and pray for seven days to draw attention to the problems in the Middle East.	John Sentamu's wife is called Margaret.
When driving in East London, John was once stopped by the police for no reason.	John Sentamu had to flee from Uganda after threats from the government.	John watched a TV news programme about the crisis in the Lebanon.
40 pilgrims joined John Sentamu on one of the days of his vigil.	John Sentamu is the 97th Archbishop of York.	Jesus taught that his followers should treat others as they would like to be treated.
John Sentamu was the first black archbishop in the Church of England.	Some people thought that the vigil was a waste of time.	John Sentamu shaved his head as a symbol of hope.
John Sentamu believed God guided him to help the people he heard about on the news.	John Sentamu was the 6th of 13 children.	John Sentamu was previously the Bishop of Birmingham.

The prophet Isaiah wandered around naked as a sign that the people would lose their land if they didn't obey God.	John Sentamu cancelled his family holiday in order to take part in the vigil.	The Prophet Ezekiel walked about with bags on his back to warn people that they would go into exile.
Jesus rode a donkey into Jerusalem as a sign of humility.	The situation in Lebanon was getting worse and many people were suffering.	John Sentamu trained as a lawyer. He became a High Court judge in Uganda.
John Sentamu wanted people to take notice of what was happening in Lebanon.	John Sentamu believed that prayer works.	John Sentamu wanted to make politicians sit up and take notice; he cancelled his holiday.
The Bible says: 'Let no one seek his own good, but the good of his neighbour.' (1 Corinthians 10: 24).	John Sentamu enjoys cooking.	John Sentamu was frustrated that politicians didn't seem to know what to do.
John Sentamu thought that acting out his beliefs would attract more attention than preaching a sermon.	In the Old Testament prophets often acted out the message God had for people.	Jesus taught that prayer and fasting was the best way of dealing with difficult situations.

9-11

Blog spot

Activity 3　Blog spot

This is a more challenging activity for pupils with higher levels of literacy ability.

Provide pupils with copies of the nine statements below – six extracts from blogs, and three quotes – all published in the *Sunday Times* at the time of John Sentamu's vigil (20 August 2006). Print them on card and cut them into separate cards, sufficient for one set for each group of pupils.

Working in small groups, ask pupils to complete one or more of the following:

- **Identify** those cards that support John Sentamu's actions and those that don't.
- **Choose** the card that comes closest to their own view – and the one that is furthest away from it.
- **Choose** one card and **write** a reply – the next part of the conversation or the next entry in the blog.
- **Compose** a short email to John Sentamu – of support or challenge.

Working individually, ask pupils to:

- **Choose** something about which they feel strongly (e.g. cruelty to animals, the war in Iraq).
- **Decide** what sort of action they would consider to draw people's attention to it. How far would they go and why?
- **Share** and **compare** ideas with the class, noticing similarities and differences of reasons and responses.

It's an amazing act. I look at him and I am shocked but impressed. It makes me think this is an important action for reconciliation in our world. *Jong Il Kim,* Sunday Times, *20 August 2006*	It depends if you believe or not. I personally think the church has had it, but my kids are impressed. *Stan, aged 31, in* Sunday Times, *20 August 2006*	I'm worried he's going to get ill with not eating. But I still think it will make a difference. *Anna, aged 18,* Sunday Times, *20 August 2006*
Rather than preach lengthy sermons some religious figures choose symbolic actions to highlight the will of God. Think of Simeon Stylite who lived on a pillar for 36 years! Although Sentamu's "prophetic enactment" is a little less extreme, it is nonetheless quite powerful.' *www.bycommonconsent.com*	This is a man who knows about Christian leadership. This is a man who goes the extra mile. *andygoodlilff.typepad.com*	This would be the same Archbishop of York with whom I so passionately disagree on so many issues. What a great reminder that the one who opposed me is not necessarily The Enemy, but a brother with whom I am in conflict. *frjakestopstheworld.blogspot.com*
He (John Sentamu) often speaks about how sorry he is that most of the world has to live in poverty. The Church of England has £5bn in the bank. *vexen.livejournal.com/285464.html*	If the Bish wants to identify with the oppressed, all he needs to do is to change into plain clothes and wander around Bradford wearing a crucifix. *ukcommentators.blogspot.com*	This is the true face of Christianity – love, compassion, humility. *www.democraticunderground.com*